the new aga cook

No1 breakfast & brunch

Also in the series

Cooking for Kids

Good Food Fast

Laura James

the new aga cook

No1 breakfast & brunch

Absolute Press

the new aga cook

First published in 2003

Text and design © Laura James 2003

Image pages 12-13 courtesy © J. Barbour & Sons
Herb images courtesy © Aga Foodservice Group

First published in the United Kingdom by
Absolute Press
Scarborough House, 29 James Street West, Bath, England BA1 IAS.
Tel: 44 (0) 1225 316013
Fax: 44 (0) 1225 445836
E-mail: office@absolutepress.co.uk
Website: www.absolutepress.co.uk

ISBN 1 904573 07 X

Photography: Andy Davis
Food styling: Penny Chambers

For Lucie and Tatiana

The perfect breakfast companions

breakfast & brunch
menu

There are few things as enjoyable as time

intro

When, recently married and impossibly young, my husband and I rented a sweet little cottage with an Aga, I fell in love with it at first sight, although I can now admit to having been slightly daunted by the thought of cooking on it.

We moved in on a Saturday and on the Sunday morning I got up and cooked a huge brunch for all the friends who'd helped us. It tasted amazing and my husband joked that I must have been taking secret cookery classes. In fact, it was simply the Aga's ability to compensate for the shortcomings of youth.

Since then, Sunday morning Aga breakfasts and brunches have become a ritual for us. For me, there are few things as enjoyable as spending time around a crowded kitchen table eating delicious food with people I adore.

For many of us, life is a battle against deadlines and cooking weekday suppers or making up lunch boxes can seem like just another chore to add to the list. Weekends, though, should be different and it's surprisingly relaxing to potter around the kitchen cooking fab food for an army of friends and family.

While I don't struggle to cook only dishes that are seasonal, the weather of course plays a part in how we eat. There's nothing like a huge brunch in the depths of winter to set you up for – or indeed to reward you for – a long,

at the kitchen table with people I adore...

bracing walk and breakfast in the garden is a fabulous treat during the summer months.

I don't profess to be a professional cook, but I do passionately love food and cooking. I'm a working mother of four and, while I buy lots of cookery books with fantastically stylish and complicated recipes, I also admit to rarely using them. I find long, drawn-out explanations befuddling and am often left feeling inadequate when I have neither the time, nor the energy to cook a four-course meal for my six-year-old and his friends.

The kitchen should be a friendly place, a bolt hole from the outside world, not somewhere one feels judged. Kitchen life – particularly when there's time to loiter – is the perfect antidote to the pressures of the modern world and, after a hard week, a bit of weekend time spent cooking really can be as relaxing as a massage or a long bath.

This book is offered in exactly that spirit. It's not for one moment meant to be a textbook to be followed to the letter. I hope you'll use it much more as an informal collection of ideas intended to inspire you to get into the kitchen and enjoy yourself!

Laura James

The kitchen should be a friendly place.

Not somewhere one feels judged…

breakfast

Francis Bacon said 'hope is a good breakfast'. It's true – there's something about the freshness of the morning, when anything's possible, and what better way to start the day than with something truly delicious…

I remember

being told over and again as a child that breakfast was the most important meal of the day.

But as I was growing up (and certainly during my teenage years) a cup of coffee and anything snatched from the pantry before I flew out the door seemed to be the order of the day.

Now I have children of my own it's really lovely to sit down for a proper family breakfast and to chat about everything that's going on.

Of course breakfast can be whatever you want it to be. But there's something elemental about starting the day with food you've prepared yourself, rather than something out of a box.

In this section I've included recipes – many of them deliberately loose and informal – for some of my

favourites

egg, bacon and sausage muffins

I hate with a passion those red and yellow fast-food outlets you see in every town. But most children don't and I have to admit that, while I don't enjoy the mass-produced version of this dish, if it's made with the very best ingredients it's really fantastic

1 egg

1 sausage

1 rasher of bacon

Half a tomato

1 English muffin

Line a roasting tin with Bake-O-Glide and place the sausages on the rack. Cook in the roasting oven on the first set of runners for about 10 minutes.

Take the tin out, turn the sausages and slide in the tomatoes underneath the rack. Cook for a further 5 minutes.

Add the bacon and cook for about 7 minutes, turning once. While this is going on, lightly grease a round piece of Bake-O-Glide and place it on the simmering plate. Break the egg on to the Bake-O-Glide and close the lid. The egg will only take a couple of minutes, so keep checking to ensure it's done just how you like it.

While the egg is cooking, toast the muffin in the Aga toaster on the boiling plate and remove the sausages, bacon and tomatoes from the roasting oven.

Butter the muffin lightly. Cut the sausage in half lengthways and place on the bottom of the muffin. Put the bacon on top, then the fried egg and, finally, the tomato. Then simply sit back and enjoy…

Makes one muffin

Enjoy a full breakfast in one truly del

Try the

chill-out pancakes

Weekends were made for children. And pancakes were made for weekends. I love making up the batter with the children and enjoying their faces as they await the first to come out of the pan…

A little butter
8 rashers of streaky bacon
115g (4 oz) of plain flour
1 teaspoon of baking powder
Pinch of salt
3 eggs, beaten
140ml (5 fl oz) of full-fat milk
Maple syrup

Fry the bacon and set aside. Sift all the dry ingredients into a large bowl and make a well. Then gradually add the eggs, slowly adding the milk as you go, until the batter is smooth. Or, if time is tight, simply blitz all the ingredients in a blender.

You can cook the pancakes directly on the simmering plate or on a round piece of Bake-O-Glide on the simmering plate, having simply smeared either with a little butter.

Place single tablespoons of batter on to the surface, allowing them room to spread. Once the pancakes puff up and start to bubble, turn them over and cook for a further minute or two.

Then simply place the pancakes in little piles on plates and criss-cross each one with the bacon.

Pour over the maple syrup and enjoy!

Serves 4

se pancakes with bananas, blueberries or

eggy bread

This was the first dish my eldest daughter attempted. I remember her frown of concentration and the look of triumph as she watched us all tucking in enthusiastically!

1 large egg
Splash of full-fat milk
2 slices of bread, preferably thick
  and slightly stale
Butter, for frying

It's hopelessly twee, I know, but my children adore Eggy Bread when it's cut into cute shapes, such as rabbits, ducks or stars.

Biscuit cutters are perfect for this job and the only limit to the shapes possible is your imagination – or, more probably, your embarrassment threshold.

Beat the egg with the milk. Soak the bread into the mixture for about a minute. Melt the butter in a frying pan on the boiling plate then move to the simmering plate.

Place the egg-soaked bread in the frying pan and fry for a couple of minutes before turning over to fry the other side for a few more.

Serves 1

strawberries – or simply a sprinkling of sugar…

the perfect bacon sandwich

Ad campaigns have been built around it. Poems have been penned in its honour. There are awards in its name. Much is made of the ultimate bacon sandwich – here's my version…

Knob of butter
3 rashers of good-quality bacon
2 slices of thick white bread

Because the Aga is always on, it's perfect for a quick bacon sandwich. I often use my kitchen like a takeaway and whip up a quick bacon sandwich to eat in the car.

Rather than using the pan juices, my husband prefers his bacon sandwich to drip with butter and be made with the thickest, freshest brown bread.

Key to getting it right is buying the very best bacon. My favourite is from Duchy Originals – the fat seems to crisp up in a way no other bacon does. Simply divine.

In a pan on the simmering plate, fry the bacon in the butter until the fat has started to turn slightly golden. Take it out of the frying pan and dip one side of the bread into the pan.

Make up the sandwich and devour. You could, of course, add ketchup or brown sauce, but personally I regard this as sacrilege.

Makes 1 sandwich

Wash it down with a huge mug of builders' tea!

devilled kidneys

Once a favoured breakfast dish, Devilled Kidneys fell out of fashion for a while. Now, they're very much back in vogue and are simply perfect for cold winter mornings

8 lambs' kidneys
25g (1 oz) of butter
2 teaspoons of Worcestershire sauce
1 tablespoon of tomato purée
1 tablespoon of lemon juice
1 tablespoon of French mustard
Pinch of cayenne pepper
Salt and freshly ground black pepper
1 tablespoon of chopped parsley

Remove the skin from the kidneys, cut them in half and cut away the cores. Heat the butter in a frying pan on the simmering plate and cook the kidneys for about three minutes on each side.

To make the sauce, mix together all the remaining ingredients, except the parsley. In the pan, pour the devil sauce over the kidneys and stir so that they are evenly coated. Sprinkle with the chopped parsley and serve with toast.

Grilled tomatoes make a fabulous accompaniment. Slice eight tomatoes, sprinkle with sea salt and freshly ground black pepper and grill at the top of the roasting oven for about 15 minutes.

Serves 4

This devillishly good sauce has many uses

baked eggs

This recipe takes a moment to put together and doesn't need any attention while it's cooking. So you can go off and have a shower or walk the dog. Whatever makes you smile…

A little butter
1 slice of Parma ham
1 egg
1 tablespoon of single cream
25g (1 oz) of grated Red Leicester
   or Cheddar cheese
Salt and pepper

Grease a ramekin dish with butter. Put the ham in the base of the dish. Break an egg into it and spoon over the cream. Top with the grated cheese, salt and pepper.

Stand the dish on a baking tray on the grid shelf on the floor of the roasting oven and cook for 15-20 minutes until the whites of the eggs are firm.

As these are cooked in individual dishes, I've listed the ingredients for one. Obviously you can make as many as you like and the method doesn't change.

Serves 1

These are delicious with a warmed granary roll

If you like mushrooms, add a few to the skewer.

breakfast kebabs

This recipe is one of my friend Patty's favourites. It's a fabulous way to encourage children to eat a proper breakfast as they tend to be wildly excited by its novelty value

6 wooden skewers
6 rashers of streaky bacon
3 sausages
24 cherry tomatoes
Olive oil (not extra virgin)
Salt and pepper

Soak the skewers in water for about five minutes; this will stop them burning in the oven and they'll stay that lovely blonde colour.

Cut each bacon rasher in half and roll up tight. Crudely slice the sausages and thread them on to the skewers with the bacon and tomatoes. Brush with a little oil and sprinkle with salt and pepper.

Cook in a roasting tin on the top set of runners of the roasting oven for about 30 minutes, turning halfway through.

Serve with hot buttered toast and scrambled eggs (see page 28).

Serves 6

The joy is you can make them up as you wish

best-ever scrambled eggs

There's something about good scrambled eggs that makes them suitable for all weathers and all moods

6 large organic eggs
50ml (2 fl oz) of double cream
2 tablespoons of chopped smoked salmon
Black pepper

I'm sure wars have started over the perfect texture for scrambled eggs. I like mine to be slightly wet and a little runny, whereas my daughter likes them to be much more formed and almost omelette-like in their texture.

Whatever your preference, it's important to use the best possible ingredients. At last count we had two dozen chickens, who seem to be prolific egg producers. But these days the supermarkets, too, offer a decent range of eggs. It's a matter of buying well. The real secret to perfect scrambled eggs is to make sure you use the right pan. Aga Shops sell an excellent Aga non-stick cast-aluminium pan which should ensure perfect results every time.

Beat together the eggs and cream. Add the black pepper and smoked salmon and pour into the pan.

Place the pan on the simmering plate for about five minutes, stirring occasionally, until you have perfectly fluffy scrambled eggs. Serve immediately.

Serves 4

We just adore these given a kick with grated

cheese and chives instead of the salmon

aga kippers

Kippers are delicious, but the smell can hang around for days. However, if you cook them in the Aga roasting oven this shouldn't be a problem and they're perfect for icy winter mornings

1 kipper
Knob of butter

I was always slightly wary of kippers – don't ask me why, perhaps I was frightened by one as a child! I also, quite wrongly, imagined them being difficult to get right, when in fact they are the easiest things in the world to cook.

My aversion turned to true love one cold morning at the Balmoral Hotel in Edinburgh. A very smart lady sitting on the next table polished off a plate in record time and then promptly ordered another. In a When Harry Met Sally moment, I demanded "what she's having" and haven't looked back since.

As soon as the first leaf falls off the first tree I'm at the fishmonger's ordering a trawler-load of kippers. There's something about eating them in cold weather that makes one feel truly cosseted. I also confess to eating them for lunch, supper and, on a particularly hard day, afternoon tea as well. How many kippers you cook is, of course, up to you. The method remains the same.

Simply add a knob of butter to each kipper, wrap in foil and place in a roasting tin. Cook on the third set of runners in the roasting oven for 15-20 minutes.
Serves 1

The Aga seems ideally suited to doing kippers.

The stored heat gives perfect results every time

aga porridge

There's something rather romantic about making up porridge late on a Saturday night, putting it in the simmering oven and coming down to it all creamy and delicious on a grey Sunday morning

600ml (20 fl oz) of water
75g (2 $^3/_4$ oz) of pinhead oatmeal
   (Hamlyns is fabulous)
Sugar to taste
Couple of tablespoons of double cream

For me, this dish will always taste of Christmas as it's the one thing I can persuade my children to eat before they start on the present opening.

Last thing at night, bring the water to the boil in a heavy-based pan and stir in the oatmeal. Bring back to the boil and then move the pan to the simmering plate for a couple of minutes. Cover the pan with a tightly fitting lid and move to the grid shelf on the floor of the simmering oven (or the warming oven in a four-oven Aga). Leave overnight. In the morning, stir well and add sugar and cream.

Of course, if you'd prefer a more authentic taste, you should forget about the sugar and cream and simply add salt.

Serves 2

We had a gardener who refused to work unless

strawberry and white chocolate muffins

These are divine. My daughters invite friends simply, I believe,

so they can eat these wonderfully sinful but wholesome delights!

30g (1 oz) of butter
3 tablespoons of vanilla syrup
1 egg
4 tablespoons of full-fat milk
Punnet of strawberries
150g (5 $^1/_2$ oz) of white chocolate
150g (5 $^1/_2$ oz) of plain flour
1 teaspoon of baking powder
$^1/_2$ teaspoon of bicarbonate of soda
6 muffin cases

Leave the butter to melt in a bowl on the top of the Aga and mix with the vanilla syrup and egg. Chop the strawberries into quarters and enjoy smashing the chocolate into small pieces!

Mix the dry ingredients in a bowl, then add the butter, vanilla syrup, egg mixture and the milk. Add the chocolate and strawberries and gently mix until you have a deliciously lumpy mulch. Put the muffin cases into a muffin tray and spoon in the mixture. With the grid shelf on the floor of the roasting oven, put in the muffin tray and cook for about 25 minutes. If the muffins start to brown too quickly, slide in the cold plain shelf on the third set of runners. In a four oven Aga, place the muffin tray on the grid shelf on the third set of runners of the baking oven. Cook for about 25 minutes.

Makes 6 muffins

he had a cup of coffee and one of these muffins!

blueberry muffins

These are muffins to die for. I often put them in the children's lunchboxes or have them with a mug of hot chocolate at bedtime. When I'm busy I serve them warm with ice cream as a pudding

350g (12 oz) of plain flour
112g (4 oz) of caster sugar
2 teaspoons of baking powder
Pinch of salt
1 egg
150ml (5 fl oz) of full-fat milk
110g (3 $^3/_4$ oz) of blueberries

In my mind at least these muffins are the staple basics of every American breakfast. When I cook them I feel like a '50s housewife waiting for her husband to leap over the picket fence with the Sunday papers, followed by a dog called Skip.

Mix the dry ingredients together, then beat in the egg, milk and butter. Gently fold in the blueberries. Put the muffin cases into a muffin tray and spoon in the mixture.

With the grid shelf on the floor of the roasting oven, put in the muffin tray and cook for 25-30 minutes.

If the muffins start to brown too quickly, slide in the cold plain shelf on the third set of runners.

In a four oven Aga, place the muffin tray on the grid shelf on the third set of runners of the baking oven. Cook for about 25 minutes.

Makes about 12

cinnamon toast

Eating this on freezing winter mornings is an abiding memory.
In my teens, a group of us used to go to a little café in Hampstead
and eat endless rounds washed down with mugs of hot chocolate…

2 thick slices of bread
Unsalted butter
$1/_2$ teaspoon of ground cinnamon
1 tablespoon of golden caster sugar

Cinnamon toast takes minutes to make.
My children all love it and I have found
them in the kitchen at some ungodly hour
making batches of it, ready for me to pop
in the Aga when I stagger downstairs.
It's blissful on cold winter mornings and
perfect as a bedtime treat. I have to admit,
I eat it at any time of day and it's a good
alternative to the plain variety.

Toast the bread on one side in the Aga
toaster. Butter the untoasted side. Mix the
cinnamon with the sugar and sprinkle it
on the buttered side of the toast.

Place the bread on a baking sheet,
buttered side up and hang on the highest
set of runners in the roasting oven.

Cook for about 30 seconds to one minute
or until the sugar has melted and has
started to bubble nicely.

Serves 1

Fabulously simple prepare-in-a-moment treats

seriously good smoothies

Not Aga recipes, I know, but too delicious to leave out.

Plus, they're so healthy you'll feel exceedingly smug having

had them for breakfast!

Juicy Smoothie

1 ripe banana
10 strawberries
1 ripe mango
250ml (9 fl oz) chilled fresh orange juice
Ice cubes

Peel the mango, removing the large stone in the middle, and slice. Slice the banana and cut the strawberries in half. Put all the ingredients, including the orange juice, into a blender and blitz until completely smooth. Pour into glasses over ice. Enjoy! Substitute vanilla soya milk for the orange juice if you fancy a change.

Serves 1

Creamy Smoothie

75ml (2 $^3/_4$ fl oz) of pineapple juice
170g (6 oz) of diced pineapple
1 chopped banana
Large scoop of vanilla ice cream
Ice cubes

Simply throw everything – including the pineapple juice – into a blender and whizz it up until completely smooth. Then pour into glasses over ice and enjoy the journey to more exotic climes.

Serves 1

just bursting with wonderful feelgood flavours…

brunch

Brunch is the perfect opportunity to catch up with friends. There's something about a slow, lazy brunch that gives you a chilled-out feeling that lasts all week…

brunch

is a real alternative when you want to get a group of friends together.

Dinner parties are wonderful, but often fiendishly difficult to arrange. There's the babysitting issue, diaries that tend to be booked up months in advance and the fag of taxis home late at night.

The great thing about a brunch party is you can fill your house with people of every age, there's little formality and everyone seems to muck in and get on with it – and each other. When you invite people for lunch, they tend to arrive just before it's served and leave shortly after the last plate is stacked in the dishwasher.

With brunch, people seem to turn up as you're cooking and potter round the kitchen. And, as there's so much of the day left when you've finished eating, you can enjoy a long walk or softball in the garden.

On the following pages, you'll find some of my family's favourites, as well as some new recipes we have tried out and enjoyed

Instead of the chives, try Avruga as a garnish…

smoked salmon blinis

My first boyfriend's mother, who was unbelievably glamorous, used to make these every Sunday morning and I can't eat them without being instantly transported back to her kitchen…

300ml (10 fl oz) of milk
6g sachet of easy-blend yeast
5ml (1 tsp) of sugar
25g (1 oz) of buckwheat flour
175g (7 oz) of strong plain flour
5ml (1 tsp) of salt
2 eggs, separated
25g (1 oz) of butter
600g (1 lb 5 $^1/_2$ oz) of smoked salmon
300ml (10 fl oz) of soured cream
Chopped chives to garnish

Gently warm the milk in a pan on the simmering plate and blend with the yeast and sugar. Leave to stand for 10 minutes. Sieve the flours and salt into a mixing bowl and make a well in the centre. Gradually beat in the milk mixture and egg yolks. Cover and leave in a warm place (on the simmering plate lid is a good place for this) for an hour.

Whisk the egg whites and fold into the batter. Lightly grease the simmering plate with butter. Spoon the mixture in tablespoons on to the simmering plate, leaving even spaces between them. Cook each side for 30 seconds.

Top each blini with smoked salmon and very cold soured cream. Garnish with chopped chives.

Makes about 12

The bold colours look really fantastic together

ham and emmental croissants

Ham and Emmental are a perfect combination. The nuttiness of the cheese goes perfectly with the slight saltiness of the ham. Add that to the sweet flakiness of the croissant and you've culinary heaven

1 slice of ham
1 fairly thick slice of Emmental
A good grind of black pepper
1 croissant

Sometimes when we're feeling really lazy on a Saturday morning we take the children out for breakfast to a fabulous café in Holt called Byfords.

Short of enjoying warm croissants and café au lait in Paris, they do the best we've had. Much better than the rubbery supermarket variety. Often, we buy a bag to bring home and on Sunday morning I'll fill them with ham and cheese and we'll eat them in the garden if the weather's being kind.

Split the croissant in two and put the ham on one side with the cheese on top. Grill that half of the croissant at the top of the roasting oven for a few minutes until the cheese has melted. It's important not to overdo them – they're undoubtedly best only lightly crisped with the cheese oozing out delightfully. Place the other half of the croissant in the oven for the last 30 seconds or so, then put the croissant back together again and enjoy!

For a cold filled croissant, try smoked salmon and cream cheese with a sprinkling of chives

Serves 1

swiss-style frittata

This recipe is simple, filling and seriously wholesome, but it doesn't taste the least bit worthy

4 potatoes, diced
$^1/_2$ an onion, sliced
1 tablespoon of vegetable oil
8 eggs, beaten
100g (3 $^1/_2$ oz) of chopped ham
Salt and freshly ground pepper to taste
100g (3 $^1/_2$ oz) of grated Emmental

On the boiling plate, bring to the boil a large pan of salted water. Add the potatoes and cook until they're tender but still firm. Drain and set aside to cool.

Heat the oil in a cast-iron frying pan on the simmering plate. Add the onions and cook slowly, stirring occasionally, until soft. Stir in the eggs, potatoes, ham, salt and pepper. Cook until the eggs are firm.

Top the frittata with the grated cheese and put the pan into the roasting oven with the grid shelf on the second set of runners until the cheese has melted.

Serves 4

You can caramelise the onions and skip the ham

ciabatta with goats' cheese and mushrooms

Perfect for an informal brunch. It takes only 15 minutes to make and is fab with a huge bowl of salad and a large glass of dry white wine

1 ciabatta loaf
60ml (2 fl oz) of olive oil
1 garlic clove, crushed
100g (3 $^1/_2$ oz) creamy goats' cheese
60ml (2 fl oz) of sun-dried tomato paste
125g (4 $^1/_2$ oz) of mushrooms,
  thinly sliced
Parsley, chopped

Cut the bread in half lengthways and then each piece in half again to make four slices. In a shallow bowl, mix the olive oil with the garlic. Press the cut side of the bread into the olive oil.

Spread each slice with the goats' cheese and the sun-dried tomato paste. Place on a baking tray and spoon over the mushrooms and the remaining oil. Cook in the roasting oven, with the grid shelf on the lowest set of runners, for about 10 minutes.

Serve immediately, garnished with parsley.

Serves 4

Try these with Mozzarella and cherry tomatoes

This is a simple but effective dish that's so good

prawn savoury

I discovered this recipe in a charming booklet called *Menus and Recipes for Aga Cookery Demonstrations*, first published in 1939. It makes a lovely light brunch

8 large prawns
8 fingers of toast
8 rashers of streaky bacon
Lemon juice
Seasoning

Shell the prawns and sprinkle with lemon juice and seasoning. Roll each prawn in a thin rasher of streaky bacon.

Lay them on a baking sheet and place them in the roasting oven for around 5-7 minutes.

Serve on fingers of hot buttered toast.

Serves 4

served with drinks before dinner… total bliss!

brunch crêpes

These crêpes are like a mini-breakfast in their own right, but unusual enough to serve as a brunch for friends. Be sure to make enough though – they have a habit of disappearing quickly!

For the crêpes
125g (5 oz) of plain flour
Large pinch of of salt
2 eggs
250ml (8 fl oz) of milk
25g (1 oz) of melted butter
Vegetable oil

Sieve all the dry ingredients into a mixing bowl and make a well in the centre. Add the eggs and half of the milk. Gradually mix together to make a smooth, thick batter. Stir in the remaining milk and the melted butter. Beat for 2-3 minutes. For each crêpe, heat 5ml of oil in a frying pan on the boiling plate until very hot and pour in a thin film of batter. Cook until it's a gorgeous golden colour, then flip over the crêpe and cook the other side. Keep it warm in the simmering oven while you make the other crêpes and the filling.

For the filling
1 egg fried to your liking
3 rashers of cooked bacon cut into small pieces
75g (3 oz) of diced sautéed potatoes
1 tbsp of parsley, chopped

To assemble
Place the crêpe on a warmed plate. Put the egg in the centre. Scatter the bacon and potatoes around the egg. Garnish with parsley.

Serves 6-8

egg and onion bagels

The staple ingredient of a deli breakfast, at home we pile the table with egg and onion, smoked salmon, cream cheese and smoked cod's roe and make up our bagels as we go along…

8 bagels
7 eggs
Five tablespoons of mayonnaise
Small bunch of spring onions, chopped
Salt and black pepper

Bring a pan of water on the boiling plate and, when it starts to bubble, move to the simmering plate and add the eggs. Leave to simmer for 8-10 minutes.

Remove the eggs from the pan and place in a bowl of ice cold water. When the eggs are cool enough, peel them. Mash the eggs in a bowl, adding the mayonnaise, spring onions, salt and pepper.

Lightly toast the split bagels using the Aga toaster on the simmering plate. Then spread the egg and onion mixture on the bagel.

Serves 4

Pile the bagels high, serve with a huge bowl of

egg and onion and let the good times roll…

One of my newly discovered favourites. Simply

ham and pepper piperade

This dish is an exquisite mix of soft scrambled eggs and slightly crunchy vegetables. The ham gives it a delicious, almost smoky quality

**150ml (5 fl oz) of olive oil
(not extra virgin)**
6 slices of Prosciutto ham
1 medium onion, finely chopped
**3 ripe tomatoes, peeled and coarsely
chopped**
1 green pepper, cut into thin strips
1 red pepper, cut into thin strips
2 cloves of garlic, minced
8 fresh eggs
50ml (2 fl oz) of double cream
Salt and freshly ground pepper

Heat the oil in a large pan on the simmering plate and sauté the ham for about two minutes. Remove and put on a plate. Sauté the onions for about five minutes. Add the tomatoes, peppers, and garlic and cook gently until almost all the juices have evaporated.

Beat together the eggs and the cream, add the salt and pepper and pour over the vegetables in the pan.

Gently stir the eggs so they don't stiffen – they should be the texture of soft scrambled egg rather than that of an omelette. Garnish with the ham before serving.

Serves 2-4

gorgeous with fresh crusty bread and a salad

details

Fish

FishWorks Direct delivers more than 24 types of fish, 10 varieties of shellfish and five smoked seafoods direct to the door. Call on 0800 0523717 or visit www.fishworks.co.uk

Meat

Donald Russell Direct offers truly wonderful meat which is vacuum packed so it lasts longer in the fridge. Call 01467 629666 or visit the website at www.donaldrussell.com

Eggs

I can't stress enough the importance of using free-range organic eggs. For Freedom Farm Eggs, call Farmaround on 020 7627 8066.

Cheese

Neals Yard Dairy on 020 7240 5700 is one of the best places to get an extensive range.

Cookware

There are Aga Shops throughout the UK stocking a comprehensive range of cookware. They also host demonstrations and events. Call 08457 125207 to be directed to your nearest store.

Aga Magazine

A quarterly title with a 16-page recipe section in every issue. To subscribe, call 01562 734040.

Agalinks

Agalinks has a huge database of recipes from a host of chefs and cookery writers, including Mary Berry and Louise Walker. It's also home to the Aga Cookery Doctor, who will answer culinary questions and offer hints for successful cooking. Visit www.agalinks.com

Useful information no cook should be without…

thanks

So many have helped with this book, that I'm terrified I'll miss someone out. But here goes. A huge thank you to…

Patty Page for all her help with ideas and recipes.

Maggie, Pauline, Linda and Jayne for lending me ovens, cookware, expertise and a shoulder when it all got too much.

Dawn Roads for her help and guidance. Simon Page for his unstinting support.

Jon Croft, Meg Avent and Matt Inwood at Absolute Press, who held my hand as I became an author and were remarkably patient throughout!

Andy and Penny for such creativity. And, lastly, my heartfelt gratitude to my husband, Tim, without whom I couldn't write a shopping list, let alone a book!

Laura

Norfolk, Autumn 2003

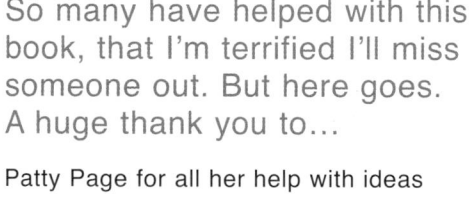